Sadie Clark

C000082896

Algorithms

Salamander Street

PLAYS

First published in 2024 by Salamander Street Ltd., a Wordville imprint. (info@salamanderstreetcom).

Algorithms Sadie Clark, 2024

Cover Image: Ali Wright Photography
Cover Design: Katie Gabriel Allen

PB ISBN: 9781738429394

10 9 8 7 6 5 4 3 2 1

Further copies of this publication can be purchased from
www.salamanderstreet.com

INTRODUCTION

In 2016 I was ready to give up acting. The whole thing felt too hard, for a number of reasons: the constant rejection, the lack of agency, frustration at still not having an agent and feeling like I didn't have access to the jobs I wanted as a result. I had applied for Soho Theatre's Writers' Lab scheme that summer, thinking perhaps I could write myself something to perform, and had been rejected. Being who I am, I decided this meant I was a terrible writer and there was no point in pursuing this avenue either, so I might as well give up...

Later that year, my sister gave me Amy Poehler's memoir *Yes Please*. Reading it reminded me why I wanted to pursue performing in the first place: I loved making people laugh. Poehler's memoir, which was full of memories of her time doing improv, prompted me to sign up to my first term of improv with Monkey Toast.

It's no exaggeration to say that improv changed my life.

It helped pull me out of the depression I was in by offering me a place where I could follow my impulses and set my inner child free—the one who had always loved making shit up and playing silly characters. I found I could get into a state of flow and play with improv that I hadn't experienced in a very long time. It reminded me that, shit, I could act!? I wasn't just good at being funny, I was good at playing the truth of a scene, and the stakes of a scene (which more often than not ended up leading to laughs). And the more I improvised, the more I wondered if maybe I could write something for myself to perform after all...

Writing had always felt so scary. It involved committing words to paper that sounded clunky and forced, and what if I got it wrong? I hadn't yet learnt about the concept of a 'shit draft', the one you get down just to have *something*, no matter how full of exposition it is. Improv gave me permission to be clunky. In the words of my first improv teacher, David Shore, it was always better to be 'super fucking clear' than clever. In improv you want to get out the who, the what and the where within your first three lines. You don't want to dance around the thing. Giving myself permission to be clunky in improv, and just get the idea out, was what gave me permission to try writing again. I started to think, "If I can make things up on stage, surely I can make them up on the page too?"

So, I decided that I would apply to Soho Theatre's Writers' Lab again, once more with the hope of writing myself a solo show to perform. This time I took part in a workshop, run by Soho Theatre's Jules Haworth, for

LGBTQ+ writers thinking of applying to the programme. I can vividly remember walking into the space. I was newly out as bisexual and I think a small part of me felt like I shouldn't really be at this workshop, given I'd only come out about six months ago and had only been in 'straight' relationships before. But I buried the feeling and proudly declared "I'm a bisexual actor hoping to write my first play" in the introductions. Jules was incredibly encouraging of my writing in that workshop, and I applied to the Writers' Lab using the piece I had written on that workshop.

I was at the Edinburgh Fringe as a punter a few months later when I got the email telling me I had been successful with my application. I remember standing in the courtyard at Summerhall thinking "This is it. I'm going to write my solo show". And I did.

If *Algorithms* was born on the Soho Theatre Writers' Lab, it was conceived from a feeling I was still struggling with of not being enough. I was still trying to work out where I fit in the Queer community, as a bisexual person who had not yet had a 'Queer' relationship. I was constantly on Facebook (it was 2017) looking at where other people were in their lives, and what they had achieved, and feeling like I was getting it all wrong. I was also desperately lonely. I was single, and felt like I didn't have any close friends. I was struggling with my mental health again, but I didn't know how to talk about it. I felt I was too much and not enough at the same time. Brooke, and her story, came from all those feelings. She is a mix of me, and other people, and pure fiction. Her story grew with invaluable input from Jules Haworth, who was my dramaturg throughout my time on the Soho Writers' Lab, and beyond. It grew further when Madelaine Moore came on board as my director in the summer of 2018.

It was thanks to Jules that *Algorithms* was programmed to be part of *Soho Rising* at Soho Theatre in December 2018. Its success at *Soho Rising* meant it felt pretty easy to secure a spot at the Edinburgh Fringe Festival 2019, which had always been my aim. *Algorithms* played at The Pleasance Courtyard for the month of August before transferring to The Pleasance London (2019) and Soho Theatre (2020 & 2021).

At the end of my run at Soho Theatre in 2021, I thought I was saying goodbye to the stage version of Brooke for good. I had been commissioned to adapt the play into a six-part audio series for Audible, which was released in 2022, and I thought that was it for the stage version of the show. Then earlier this year, Maddy and Laura approached me to see if I wanted to do a four week run of *Algorithms* at the Park Theatre. A four-week run had always been the long-term goal, but one which was somewhat scuppered by Covid, and lockdown hitting two days after my 2020 run at Soho Theatre ended. But did I want to bring back a story I had written more than six years ago now...?

I thought about it for a week, talking to various people I trusted, before deciding I was genuinely excited about bringing the show back, and stepping into Brooke's shoes once more. But me being me, I didn't want to perform the same show I had written six years ago. I wanted to use what I'd learnt as a writer since to make it even better. There have been times over the last few months when I've kicked myself for deciding I was going to redraft it ahead of this run. The show sold out all its previous runs! It won awards! I was in The Guardian for God's sake! But I'm so glad I decided to push through in order to present this (slightly) newer version of Brooke...

I have loved stepping back into her shoes, and I hope you enjoy the show, and/or reading her story.

Sadie Clark
2024

ACKNOWLEDGEMENTS

Jules, you have been with me on every step of this journey, and I cannot thank you enough for your support and belief in me. Not only are you a brilliant dramaturg, you are also a brilliant friend. I am incredibly grateful to have you in my life and this show would not have achieved what it did without you. Thank you, thank you, thank you.

Maddy, thank you for shaping Brooke and this show from the very beginning. You've been integral to creating this goofy, loveably hapless person I adore playing. Also, thanks for making me write more of Lucinda into the story way back in 2018. The show would most certainly have less laughs (and tears) without her and her Whatsapp messages.

Molly, I know you joined me and Brooke very recently, but I am eternally grateful for your input on this version of the show. For pushing me to keep going with the redrafts, even when I was losing the will, and for helping this perfectionist to unlock her new perfect (!?) ending.

Laura, thank you for being the cool as a cucumber producer everyone needs, and keeping me sane and grounded when I'm spiralling into worrying about everything.

Jess, Eva, Rosanna, Nneka and Sophie, I'm so grateful to have you as my Queers.

Becky, thank you for shouting about the show with the biggest, bestest proud sister energy a girl could ask for, rallying so many people to come along over the years, and sitting through the show so many times yourself (10 and counting!)

Mum and Dad, I'm incredibly lucky to have had your support over the years as I left my sensible Science degree behind and tried to carve out a career in 'the arts'... It's meant financial stability in a sector where, depressingly, if you are not fortunate enough to have that help, it's a million times harder to make your own work, or survive as a writer/actor/creative (for the love of God, our government should be properly funding the arts!) On top of that, you've supported me emotionally, driven me and the set around on tour, watched the dog for me when I was rehearsing, handed out flyers in Edinburgh, shared the Edinburgh Crowdfunder, sat in the audience yourselves multiple times (yes Dad, you have seen it the most out of everyone), told your friends to come and see it... the list goes on. Thank you so much for all that you've done and continue to do to support me.

Alex, you are the love of my life and I'm extremely relieved that you decided to start eating cheese a few weeks after we met otherwise I don't know if it would have worked out... Thank you for supporting me through the overwhelm and stress of redrafting this play whilst juggling my 'money jobs', and the last minute publishing of the script, on top of everything else I've had going on over the last few months. I love our life together and I'm so very lucky to have you to dance in the kitchen with after a hard day.

And finally, to every audience member who has seen this show, who's laughed and cried, and told me what *Algorithms* meant to them. Your responses to it are what kept me going through all the times of self-doubt (cos I'm still working on that...).

Algorithms was first performed on 12th December 2018 at Soho Theatre with Sadie Clark in the role of Brooke. It was performed at the Edinburgh Fringe Festival in 2019 before transferring to Pleasance London (2019) and Soho Theatre (2020 and 2021). In 2024 it transferred to Park Theatre for a four-week run with the following cast and creatives.

CAST

Brooke: **Sadie Clark**

CREATIVES

Writer: **Sadie Clark**

Director: **Madelaine Moore**

Producer: **Laura Elmes—Wild Park Entertainment**

Lighting Desginer: **Jennifer Rose**

Composer/Sound
Designer: **Nicola T. Chang**

Dramaturgs: **Jules Haworth & Molly Naylor**

Stage Manager/Show
Operator: **Josephine Shipp**

ABOUT THE CAST AND CREATIVES

Sadie Clark | Actor *(Brooke)* & Playwright

Sadie is a queer, bisexual, neurodivergent actor, writer and improviser based in London, with a base in Greater Manchester and South Norfolk. She gained a first in Natural Science from the University of East Anglia in 2012 before doing what any sensible girl would do, and moving to London to train as an actor.

As an actor Sadie has performed at Soho Theatre, Pleasance Courtyard, Omnibus Theatre, The Nottingham Playhouse and the Mercury Theatre. As a writer she has been part of the Soho Theatre Writers Lab (2018), The Mercury Theatre Writer's Programme (2022) and High Tide's 'New Writer's Week' at the New Wolsey Theatre (2022). She was also one of the BFI Network x BAFTA Crew in 2021.

Her debut play, *Algorithms*, sold out at the Edinburgh Fringe (2019), where it was a best of the festival pick in The Guardian. It transferred to Soho Theatre in March 2020 and December 2021, where it also sold out. *Algorithms* won the TV Foundation's Netflix Supported 'Stage to Screen' New Voice Award, and was longlisted for the Tony Craze Award (2018). In 2021 it was commissioned for adaptation into a six-part original audio series for Audible, starring Sadie alongside Alison Steadman, Desiree Birch and Joe Thomas. This audio adaptation, released in 2022, was shortlisted for the BBC Audio Drama Awards and won a Silver ARIAS for 'Best Drama' in 2023.

Sadie was named one of The Guardian's '12 Theatre Stars of 2020' where they cited *Algorithms* as 'astonishingly assured and practically broadcast-ready... sweet, sad and, as performed by Clark herself, full of heart–with more than a touch of Miranda Hart too'.

Sadie is also trained in long-form improv with Monkey Toast, Hoopla and the Free Association. She has been improvising for eight years and gigs regularly as improv duo *A Little Bit of Tender*, and with the Queer female/non-binary improv group *Hell Yeah!* Her latest sketch *Picky* stars Alison Steadman. Her sketch *Did you say I'm a Survivor?* won the Comedy Crowd Chorts 'Judges Award' in 2021.

Madelaine Moore | Director

Madelaine is an award-winning stage and screen director. Twice shortlisted for the Sir Peter Hall Director's Award and once of the Old Vic 12 in 2021, her work is informed by her interest in disrupting traditional gendered narratives, and tackling big ideas through a feminist lens in surprising and irreverent ways through playfulness with form or subverting common tropes.

Her debut short film as writer and director, *Twitching* was selected for multiple international film festivals including BAFTA & BIFA qualifying, and won Audience Choice for Best UK Film at Poppy Jasper IFF in 2023.

Theatre credits include: *Glacier* (Old Fire Station), *Edith* (Lowry & Theatr Clwyd), *Gobble Gobble Gobble Gobble Goblin* (Old Vic Theatre), *Ladykiller* (National Tour, Brits Off Broadway), *Evelyn* (Mercury Theatre, Southwark Playhouse), *Second Person Narrative* (Arcola Theatre), *The Awakening* (Jack Studio), *FATTY FAT FAT* (Soho Theatre, Origins Award winner), *Santi & Naz* (Pleasance Theatre, Charlie Hartill winner).

Laura Elmes - Wildpark Entertainment | Producer

Wildpark Entertainment is an award-winning London-based entertainment company founded by producer Laura Elmes. Current and recent productions include *Unfortunate: The Untold Story of Ursula the Sea Witch* (Underbelly London, Underbelly Edinburgh 2019 & 2022, UK tours 2022 & 2024); *Tim Murray is Witches* (Underbelly Edinburgh); *Sophie Santos is Codependent* (Underbelly Edinburgh), *Clown Sex* (Pleasance Edinburgh); *Live at Wembley Park Theatre* with shows headlined by Sindhu Vee and Phil Wang and *Waiter! There's a Murder in My Soup* (both Troubadour Wembley Park Theatre); *Algorithms* (Pleasance Edinburgh, Soho Theatre, Park Theatre - now an Amazon Audible Original series); *Voldemort and the Teenage Hogwarts* (Assembly Edinburgh, King's Head Theatre and UK tours); *Ladykiller* (UK tour); *Vulvarine* (Assembly Edinburgh and UK tour); *Beauty and the Beast: A Gender Swapped Musical Parody* (King's Head Theatre and UK tour); *The Prophetic Visions of Bethany Lewis* (Underbelly Edinburgh and Brighton Fringe); *Tom and Bunny Save the World* (Assembly Edinburgh and UK tour) and *Buzz the Musical* (Pleasance Edinburgh and UK tour).

Jennifer Rose | Lighting Designer

Jennifer Rose is a lighting designer based in London. She lit Handel's *Acis and Galatea* for English National Opera Studio live productions. She was nominated for an Offie Theatre Award for her lighting for *The Awakening* at the Brockley Jack theatre in 2016.

Jennifer lit *Coconut*, a play by Guleraana Mir and produced by The Thelmas, which premiered at Ovalhouse Theatre before going on a nationwide tour in 2023. She also worked with The Thelmas on *Ladykiller* by Madeline Gould, which completed successful sold out runs at the Edinburgh Festival 2019 and Vaults Festival 2019. *Ladykiller* was awarded the VAULT Festival 2019 Pleasance Award, given to a show of outstanding quality across Pleasance venues.

Other lighting credits include *Now We Are Three*, by Descent Theatre, and *Goddess* by Serena Haywood performed at the Brighton Fringe Festival and at Manchester 503 Theatre.

She also worked at English National Opera as a lighting technician for a number of years. Jenny lives in East London and when not in a theatre can often be found in her art studio. She completed a Masters in Illustration in 2022.

Nicola T. Chang | Composer/Sound Designer

Nicola T. Chang is an award-winning composer/sound designer for stage and screen. She was the composer/sound designer on the 2020/21 Old Vic 12 cohort and a current BAFTA Connect Member (film composer). She was a co-winner of the Evening Standard Future Theatre Fund (Audio Design) in 2021, and has received four Off West-End Award nominations in Sound Design.

As a performer, she plays Keys 2/Percussion in *Fantastically Great Women Who Changed the World* (UK Tour), and appeared in *Six the Musical* (West End) as deputy MD/Keys 1 and in *STOMP* (West End/World Tour). She has performed with the Chineke! Orchestra, the Women of the World Orchestra and the London Film Music Orchestra.

She also works extensively in audio plays and radio dramas including *Fully Amplified Podcast Series* for Futures Theatre (Silver Award Winner British Podcast Awards 2022) co-created *Mooncake* with Isabella Leung (45North's *Written on the Waves* 2021), and co-created *Sonic Phở* with Anna Nguyen in 2022.

Selected theatre credits include: *For Black Boys Who Have Considered Suicide When the Hue Gets Too Heavy* (Garrick West End/Apollo West End/Royal Court Jerwood Downstairs/New Diorama), *My Neighbour Totoro* (RSC/Barbican), *Kerry Jackson* (National Theatre), *The Swell* (Orange Tree Theatre), *A Playlist for the Revolution* (Bush Theatre), *The Real and Imagined History of the Elephant Man* (Nottingham Playhouse/Blackpool Grand/Coventry Belgrade), *Minority Report* (Nottingham Playhouse/Birmingham Rep/Lyric Hammersmith), *TRIBE, Of the Cut* (Young Vic), *The Ministry of Lesbian Affairs* (Soho Theatre), *Little Baby Jesus* (Orange Tree Theatre), *Feral Monster* (National Theatre of Wales/Wales National Tour), *Top Girls* (Liverpool Everyman), NEST (LEEDS 2023), *Macbeth* (Leeds Playhouse), *Derren Brown's Unbelievable* (Criterion West End/Mercury Colchester/Manchester Palace), *All Mirth and No Matter* (RSC), *Dziady* (Almeida), *White Pearl* (Royal Court Jerwood Downstairs), *Miss Julie* (Chester Storyhouse), *The Death of Ophelia* (Shakespeare's Globe), *Funeral Flowers* (UK Tour/Camden Roundhouse/ Hackney Empire), *Summer Rolls* (Park), *From Shore to Shore* (Manchester Royal Exchange/UK Tour), *No Man's Land* (Square Chapel Halifax) and *A Hundred Words for Snow* (Arcola).

Selected film credits include: *If You Only Knew* (2024), *Mei* (Sundance 2022), *Baked Beans* (2022), *Twitching* (2022), *The Fight in the Dog* (2022), *The Bicycle* (2022), *Devi* (2022), *IRL* (2021), *LAID* (2021), *Getting Away with Murder(s)* (2021), *Seafruit* (2020), *A Dose of Happiness* (2019), *Boundaries* (2019), *You Wouldn't Adam and Eve It* (2019), *Postcards from the 48%* (2018) and *The Perfect Dinner* (2017).

Jules Haworth | Dramaturg

Jules is a queer and disabled dramaturg and Access Support Worker, with a focus on supporting and developing emerging writers and artists. As Creative Engagement Associate at Soho Theatre, she co-runs the prestigious Writers' Lab programme, and has run playwriting workshops and talks with Talawa Theatre, Graeae, Rich Mix, LGBTQ+ Arts, Sour Lemons, Gendered Intelligence, Traverse Theatre, Live Theatre, National Youth Theatre, Somerset House and in schools and colleges across London.

As a dramaturg, Jules has worked on award-winning plays including *Brute* by Izzy Tennyson (Underbelly), *Muscovado* by Matilda Ibini (Theatre 503 and tour) *Villain* by Martin Murphy (Underbelly, Kings Head Theatre), *On the Edge of Me* by Yolanda Mercy (Soho Theatre and UK Tour), *Quarter Life Crisis* by Yolanda Mercy (Soho Theatre and international Tour), *Wonderboy* by Ross Willis (Bristol Old Vic), *Dust* by Milly Thomas (Soho Theatre, Trafalgar Studios), *Algorithms* by Sadie Clark (Pleasance, Soho Theatre, Park Theatre) and *Little Miss Burden* by Matilda Ibini (Bunker Theatre).

Jules also co-runs the networking group Theatre Queers and is a board member for Milk Presents. Her play *Pigeon Steps* was longlisted for the Adrian Pagan Award 2014.

Molly Naylor | Dramaturg

Molly Naylor is an award-winning writer, performer and creative mentor. She is the co-creator of Sky One comedy *After Hours*. Her plays have been toured nationally and broadcast on BBC Radio 4, and she has performed her poetry and storytelling shows at festivals and events all over the world. Her third poetry collection *Whatever You've Got* is published by Bad Betty Press.

Josephine Shipp | Stage Manager/Show Operator)

Josephine Shipp is a freelance Creative Producer and Production Manager.

Recent Production Manager/TSM Credits Include: *Medusa's First Kiss* (Little Angel Theatre, 2024), *Becoming John Travulva* (Pleasance Edinburgh, Soho Theatre, 2023/4), *Godot Is A Woman* (Pleasance Edinburgh, 2022/3), *Glamrou: From Quran To Queen* (Soho Theatre, Pleasance London, 2021/3), *Andromeda* (Camden People's Theatre, 2021), *Jordan Brookes: I've Got Nothing* (Soho Theatre, Amazon Prime, Pleasance Edinburgh, 2020/21), *Collisions*: Phd Practice Festival RCSSD (2019-Present), *Algorithms* (Soho Theatre London, Pleasance Edinburgh, Tour, Park Theatre, 2019/24).

Josephine is co-director of Queer Diary CIC, a company which runs events where LGBTQ+ adults connect with their younger selves by sharing extracts from their teenage diaries (and other writing) for a friendly queer audience, in the spirit of nostalgia, celebration and queer solidarity.

ABOUT PARK THEATRE

Park Theatre was founded by Artistic Director, Jez Bond and Creative Director Emeritus, Melli Marie. The building opened in May 2013 and, with nine West End transfers, two National Theatre transfers and 15 national tours in its first ten years, quickly garnered a reputation as a key player in the London theatrical scene. Park Theatre has received six Olivier nominations, won numerous Off West End Offie Awards, and won The Stage's Fringe Theatre of the Year and Accessible Theatre Award.

Park Theatre is an inviting and accessible venue, delivering work of exceptional calibre in the heart of Finsbury Park. We work with writers, directors and designers of the highest quality to present compelling, exciting and beautifully told stories across our two intimate spaces.

Our programme encompasses a broad range of work from classics to revivals with a healthy dose of new writing, producing in-house as well as working in partnership with emerging and established producers. We strive to play our part within the UK's theatre ecology by offering mentoring, support and opportunities to artists and producers within a professional theatre-making environment.

Our Creative Learning strategy seeks to widen the number and range of people who participate in theatre, and provides opportunities for those with little or no prior contact with the arts.

In everything we do we aim to be warm and inclusive; a safe, welcoming and wonderful space in which to work, create and visit.

★★★★★ "A five-star neighbourhood theatre." Independent

As a registered charity [number 1137223] with no public subsidy, we rely on the kind support of our donors and volunteers. To find out how you can get involved visit parktheatre.co.uk

FOR PARK THEATRE

Artistic Director Jez Bond
Executive Director Catherine McKinney

Creative Engagement

Community Engagement Manager Carys Rose Thomas

Development

Head of Development Ama Ofori-Darko
Development & Producing Coordinator Ellen Harris

Finance

Finance Director Elaine Lavelle
Finance Officer Nicola Brown
Finance Assistant Pinar Kurdik

General Management

General Manager Tom Bailey
Deputy General Manager David Hunter
Producer Programmer Amelia Cherry
Administrator Mariah Sayer
Access Coordinator David Deacon
Duty Venue Managers Leiran Gibson, Zara Naeem, Laura
Riseborough, Shaun Joyson, Wayne Morris

Park Pizza

Supervisors Luke Brock, Jahmar Bennett
Park Pizza & Bar Team George Gehm, John Burman, Bradly Doko,
Hugo Harrison, Alex Kristoffy, Julia Skinner, Maddie Stoneman,
Eliyas Swart, Sion Watkins, Jessie Williams, Maria Ziolkowska

Sales & Marketing

Sales & Marketing Director Dawn James
Head of Ticketing Matthew Barker
Marketing Officer Anna Charlesworth
Marketing Assistant Conor Gormally
Senior Box Office Supervisor Natasha Green
Box Office Supervisors Jacquie Cassidy, Belinda Clark, Gareth Hackney, Trelawny Kean, Kyanne Smith, Maddie Stoneman
Public Relations Mobius Industries

Technical & Building

Technical & Buildings Manager Gianluca Zona
Interim Deputy Technical & Buildings Manager Laurl Marks
Venue Technician Michael Bird

Trustees

Ibukun Alamutu
Kurt Barling
Hedda Beeby
Anthony Clare - Chair
Jonathan Edwards
Kathleen Heycock
Bharat Mehta
Joe Smith
Julia Tyrrell

Associate Artist Mark Cameron
Creative Director Emeritus Melli Marie
Founding President Jeremy Bond (1939–2020)

With thanks to all of our supporters, donors and volunteers.

Sadie Clark

Algorithms

For all the Brookes, and their busy, busy brains.

CHARACTERS

BROOKE
(29)

NOTES ON THE PLAY

BROOKE tells the whole story. She should have specific opinions about the people she impersonates as she tells it.

The set can be as detailed or abstract as the director and designer wish.

Cultural references in the text may be updated for future performances where relevant.

NOTE ON THE TEXT

A dash — indicates an interruption or an interrupted thought.

A single full stop . indicates a shift in energy or a change of location/time.

Ellipses ... indicates a trailing off in thought, or a hesitation to speak.

1. A BEGINNING

(BROOKE emerges. Neat, ready to get it right, the telling of this story.)

BROOKE: I'm at work when she calls. She never calls me at work so I know something must have happened.

LUCINDA: Brooke, it's your Mother.

BROOKE: I know, Mum, it comes up on my phone when you call.

LUCINDA: Oh. Are you sitting down?

BROOKE: Yeah. Why?

LUCINDA: I don't know how to say this...

BROOKE: What's happened?

LUCINDA: There's been an incident...

BROOKE: My mind starts racing through scenarios: the house has burnt down, our dog Lulu's died, Dad's had a stroke–he's got cancer–Mum's got cancer! Oh my God! They're getting a divorce!?

LUCINDA: Are you sure you're sitting down?

BROOKE: Yes. What's happened?

LUCINDA: Well... there are some pictures of your bum online.

BROOKE: What?

LUCINDA: Pictures, of your bum, in lacy pants. Online.

BROOKE: What? Where online? What do you mean?

LUCINDA: On Google.

BROOKE: Why were you Google-searching my bum?

LUCINDA: Don't be ridiculous Brooke! I was on that email you sent about writing to my MP and a message popped up from the Gmail saying 'Brooke has shared some photos', so I clicked on them and when I scrolled through your bum came up.

Several times actually.

BROOKE: Oh, God.

I've taken multiple pictures of my arse: arse in grey lace French knickers, arse in a black satin thong, arse with a butt plug in—oh shit...

Has she seen 'Arse With a Butt Plug In'?

LUCINDA: Why were you taking pictures of your bum?

BROOKE: I um, I sent them to Amira.

LUCINDA: Oh. But why did you put them online?

BROOKE: I didn't put them online.

LUCINDA: Well, they're there. I'm looking at them right now.

BROOKE: Right, well could you *stop* looking at them?

LUCINDA: I just thought you should know because it's your work email address.

BROOKE: Fuck!

I log in to Gmail. Open Google plus.

Every photo I've ever taken has been shared online with *all* my contacts.

My boss... All my colleagues... Everyone.

I start furiously deleting the offending images, wondering how the fuck this happened because I *don't* make mistakes.

Pick up my new phone. Open settings, photos, 'back up and sync: ON'.

I'm hit with a vivid memory of my phone asking if I wanted to back up and sync my photos. I thought they were backing up and syncing somewhere private in case I dropped my phone down the loo. I didn't think they were syncing to my public

Google Plus account.

I look around the office, wondering who's seen them. Did Gareth just lick his lips at me?

Oh no, he's just got Tibetan momos for lunch.

Maybe it's fine. It's fine, right? It's like that bit in every romcom where something embarrassing happens to the lead and then they immediately meet the love of their life. Except I've already met mine...

Amira.

I tell her about the bum fiasco when we're in bed together later that night.

AMIRA: So? It's not like she hasn't seen your bum before.

BROOKE: Yeah, but this was my bare bum with a butt plug in it!

AMIRA: Yeah. I guess that is quite bad.

BROOKE: And then she rolls over, turning her back on me, and switches the light out.

We haven't had sex in ages. We used to do it all the time. She couldn't keep her hands off me.

Once, I was making this chickpea stew, and I turned with a spoonful of it for her to taste, but instead we started kissing. And next thing I know the spoon's clattering to the floor and she's got me up on the kitchen table, pulling my knickers down, kissing up the inside of each of my thighs, getting closer and closer to my cunt, until she's there, running her tongue up and down, and then she starts sucking my clit and I don't know if she used her teeth but there was like this pressure round it, like a love bite, and she kept sucking and sucking until my head exploded.

I was looking up at the ceiling but suddenly it was like this dark, inky sky and all these tiny pin pricks of light—stars—popping into being and I took this deep breath in, and the smells of the cooking turmeric and coconut filled my nostrils and it—was–bliss...

I think maybe that was when I first realised that I loved her.

But I don't know if that was just the orgasm talking. We'd only been dating for two weeks.

When I wake up the next day, Amira's already left for work. That's new.

I lie in bed, looking up at the ceiling. There's a tiny patch of damp on it.

2. AN ENDING

BROOKE: I'm sat at my desk in the open plan office of SlideHustle, the start-up I work for—we're developing a new dating app—when I see my boss, Katya, striding towards me. Quickly close the TikTok I was watching—'Five Minutes of Cats Jumping at Cucumbers'—before she arrives at my desk.

KATYA: Brooke, can you join me in my office for a minute?

BROOKE: Sure.

KATYA: I had a complaint this morning from Gareth. He says that you sent him some rather inappropriate photos for the work environment. I shouldn't have to remind you that we do not tolerate sexual harassment of any kind in this office. That includes sending colleagues images of a sexual nature—

BROOKE: I didn't—

KATYA: I'm issuing you with a verbal warning. Any further incidents and I will have to give you a caution in writing. Is that clear?

BROOKE: Yes. And I'm really pleased the office takes sexual harassment claims so seriously but honestly Katya, I didn't mean to send those pictures. It's my new phone. They were actually pictures I'd taken to send to my girlfriend but—

KATYA: Your girlfriend?

BROOKE: Yes.

KATYA: You have a girlfriend?

BROOKE: Yeah...

KATYA: But you're obsessed with that DJ guy?

BROOKE: Greg James? Yeah, I mean he's so silly and fun but he's also really warm and humble, like I just see him as someone who really isn't arrogant even though he's actually really attractive. And tall. I just think he'd make a really good husband—

KATYA: He's a man?

BROOKE: Yeah.

KATYA: (*still confused*) Oh...

BROOKE: Um, I'm bisexual.

KATYA: Oh, so you're one of the greedy ones.

BROOKE: No? I just like the green M&Ms as well as the blue ones—not in like a binary way, I will happily eat a non-binary M&Ms and a trans M&M is an M&M you know so yeah, OK, I will eat any of the M&Ms that I like the look of but that doesn't mean I'm going to eat all of them, right, like I'm not going to scoff the whole bag and say 'you can't have any' and I'm only eating one M&M at the moment aren't I? Although I haven't really been eating her recently but anyway what I'm saying is there's only one M&M I've eaten in the last year and that's not greedy, right? Not that it would even be greedy to eat multiple M&Ms, like, have a bag of M&Ms if you want to have a bag of M&Ms, obviously, ideally, you're like eating them in an ethical way, like ethically non-monogamous way, but crack on, right? Like that's your choice.

(*Beat.*)

KATYA: You can leave now.

•

BROOKE: When I get home Amira's watching the football.
United are losing which means she'll be in a right stinker.
ONE NIL.
They could pull it back...
They don't. Arsenal win four-nil.

It's the men's team playing by the way... Mary Earps would never. (*to AMIRA*) D'you want a beer?

AMIRA: I'm going out.

BROOKE: Oh. I thought we were ironically watching The Ultimatum: Queer Love tonight?

AMIRA: Ah tits, I forgot. Lola's having birthday drinks.

BROOKE: Oh.

AMIRA: Sorry babe, but it is her twenty-seventh.

BROOKE: Right.
Will you be back late?

AMIRA: No.

.

BROOKE: It's four AM and she's still not home.

I Whatsapp her.
'You alright?'
Watch as it turns to two blue ticks.
Wait for it to change to 'typing'.
She goes offline.
Try her mobile.

(*The phone rings.*)

No answer—she comes back online. Call her again.

(*The phone rings.*)

Nothing, but she's still online.

.

I must have fallen asleep but when I wake up the bed beside me is still cold.

I'm in bed, re-watching Bridget Jones and eating a cheesy marmite crumpet when I finally hear her key in the door. It's like, eleven AM now.

Where have you been?

AMIRA: I stayed at Lola's.

BROOKE: Why didn't you call? Or text?

AMIRA: It were a spurra the moment thing.

BROOKE: I messaged you. You were online. You saw it. I was calling you. I didn't know what had happened. I nearly rang the police!

(A look to the audience... she didn't...)

Well?

AMIRA: God, Brooke I can't deal with this right now I'm too hungover. We ended up going to Femme Fraoche, I got too drunk, my phone were dying, Lola lives just down the road from Superstore, so I stayed there.

BROOKE: Fine. I'm just glad you're back.

Her face is all scrunched up...

AMIRA: I can't do this anymore.

BROOKE: What?

AMIRA: It's not working.

BROOKE: It's—what's not working? If something's not working, then we should work out what's not working and fix it.

AMIRA: It just doesn't feel right anymore.

BROOKE: She starts stuffing clothes into her gym bag.

AMIRA: I'll come move the rest of my stuff out later this week.

BROOKE: So that's it? You're just moving out? Where are you gonna go?

AMIRA: I'll probably stay at Lola's for a bit.

BROOKE: And it hits me. Fuck. She's actually ending this. She's gonna walk out that door and that's it. She's done. And I didn't even see it coming.

Which has totally fucked my five-year plan.

3. A BROKEN HEART

BROOKE: I listen to 'All By Myself'. On repeat. Open Vinted (fast fashion isn't good for the environment) and I hit 'buy now' again and again and again and again, and when I finally stop, I realise nearly four hours have passed and I feel a bit strange. Like a new jumper isn't enough.

.

Going in to work on Monday is unbearable.

It feels like I'm barely holding the hundreds of thousands of tiny pieces I've shattered into together and that the slightest knock to my memory: a song we listened to, the Northern Line, shopping bags from Sports Direct, could shatter me again.

You know that feeling?

.

When I get into the office, I log into the SlideHustle system and start analysing our latest user feedback. It's just a minimum viable product at this stage. We're testing the idea with real users before our next investment pitch. Our USP is that we're a dating app which optimises finding love... you can design your own application for potential matches to complete, so you can filter out anyone who doesn't meet your non-negotiables, set your own KPIs and rate your dates–it's the Air BnB of love... that's what Katya wants our tagline to be anyway. Don't judge me. I got laid off when the cost of living crisis started, and I needed something fast.

Right, positive user feedback for the pitch...

(She looks at her laptop, reading.)

Nat, twenty-eight: I'm a busy and incredibly successful #girlboss with an active lifestyle, so finding the time to date has always been hard. SlideHustle helped me easily meet my dating targets, and without it I never would have met Ian. He makes me feel beautiful and cherished even in my most ugly and unlovable moments and I'm so incredibly lucky to have met him...

(BROOKE is sobbing by now.)

I should not be reading these today

KATYA: How are you getting on?

BROOKE: *(wiping away her tears)* I'm OK. I mean break-ups are always tough but—

KATYA: I meant how are you getting on with the user feedback?

BROOKE: Oh, right, yeah, no, um, yeah good.

KATYA: I want someone to talk about their personal experience of online dating in the pitch. Investors love that shit. I want you to do it.

BROOKE: Oh um, I've not—I mean I've never... online dated.

(She breaks away.)

I wanted to find love like in the movies. Two different hands reaching for the same pair of black cashmere gloves whilst Christmas shopping. I wanted orange juice spilt on a white shirt and "I'm just a girl, standing in front of a boy, asking him to love her". I wanted The Notebook: an attraction so fierce they'd threaten to throw themselves off a Ferris Wheel if I didn't go out with them.

The first time I saw Amira I was standing at the bar at 'Butch Please!'. It was fucking rammed (it always is) but I'd finally managed to slip into a gap at the front and was trying to make eye contact with one of the bar staff when I felt someone slide in next to me, grab the bartender's attention and shout out—

AMIRA: Three double Gin and Tonics.

BROOKE: I turned, ready to lay into whoever had the audacity to push in, but when I locked eyes with her my heart leapt into my mouth.

AMIRA: Shit, sorry were you next?

BROOKE: No, it's fine, you go.

AMIRA: Shit, no, I didn't mean to push in. What do you want? I'll buy yours.

BROOKE: (*smiling goofily*) A Moscow Mule please.

My very own Nora Ephron Meet Cute. Just like I'd been waiting for. That's how you find romance. Not through a spreadsheet.

(BROOKE is brought back to reality.)

KATYA: You've never online dated?

BROOKE: No.

KATYA: Well, you're single now, aren't you? Get on the app and write something about your experience for the pitch.

BROOKE: (*to the audience*) Is that even legal?

4. A TOO TIGHT DRESS

BROOKE: I've arranged to meet Mum in some designer dress shop.

She's organising this massive party for her Ruby Wedding Anniversary with my Dad. Their anniversary is the same day as my birthday. Which is either the most amazing coincidence if you're my Mum, or the worst fucking luck if you're me.

She's been trying to arrange a joint celebration for the last fifteen years. I managed to avoid 'Pearl' because it was only my twentieth. But there was no escaping 'Ruby' coinciding with my Thirtieth Birthday.

So, we're doing a BIG. JOINT. PARTY.

There's going to be a marquee. And a band. And it's black tie. So tonight, we're picking out—

LUCINDA: An appropriate party dress.

BROOKE: I turn up late. My eyes are all swollen from having a post-work cry in the office toilets.

LUCINDA: You look awful. What's happened?

BROOKE: Nothing.

(Beat.)

(BROOKE takes a breath.)

Amira broke up with me.

LUCINDA: Well, come on, chin up! Let's buy you something pretty.

•

BROOKE: In the changing rooms I try to wriggle into one of the dresses Mum's picked out. It's a size fourteen so it should fit, but it won't pull up over my arse and hips.

Try on a couple more.

None of them fit properly.

The last dress is the only one I can squeeze into. I look ridiculous. Like an oversized Disney Princess. But I'm trying to keep Mum happy.

It is just a bit too tight around the chest though. I'll have to try it in a size sixteen.

(BROOKE steps out of the changing room.)

LUCINDA: No, it's too tight.

BROOKE: Yes, thank you, I know.

(to the assistant) Can I try this in a size sixteen please?

SHOP ASSISTANT: We don't stock plus sizes.

(Beat.)

LUCINDA: Do you think you ought to try and lose a bit of weight before the party? I lost a stone and a half at Weight Watchers.

BROOKE: Yeah, and you spent the entire time counting calories and weighing yourself. I've got better things to do with my time.

(Beat.)

Back in the changing room I take the dress off and stare at myself in the mirror.

At my thighs. My hips. My belly. All the soft parts of me I hate thanks to her and growing up in a world where fat is one of the worst things you could be.

I know I'm not fat. I do know that. On like a logical level I know my body benefits from thin privilege. But I still feel like a fucking whale when she makes comments like that.

And then I hate myself because I know I'm not supposed to talk about my body like that.

I'm meant to be part of a new generation of women who've learnt how to love themselves.

But I don't.

Instead, I spend half my life hating my body, and the other half hating myself for *not* being able to love myself just the way I am.

It's such *fun*.

5. A BETRAYAL

BROOKE: When I get home, I lie on our bed, though I guess it's just my bed now, listening to the silence of the flat around me. I think the patch on the ceiling is getting bigger.

I start scrolling through WhatsApp.

(*texting*) Hey, what you up to this weekend? Fancy going out?

JOSIE: Sorry babe, me and Lex are in Hebden Bridge.

BROOKE: Classic.

(*texting*) You free this weekend?

ROSA: I've got work. Sad face. This month is soooo busy! Let's get a date in for next month? It's been ages!

(*Beat.*)

BROOKE: I thought I'd have F.R.I.E.N.D.S when I grew up. I do have friends, but not capital letters 'F.R.I.E.N.D.S', you know? A group of six who hang out every weekend and have in jokes and go on group holidays. The sort of group who'll swoop in with a box of tissues, chocolate and a bottle of wine as soon as you need picking up.

I'm on the edge of groups like that. But I've always felt like I was on the outside looking in.

Even with Amira.

Sometimes I thought if she'd just watch some of the romcoms I grew up on she might understand me more, but she always said:

AMIRA: I refuse to watch anything shit.

BROOKE: I watch all the true crime documentaries you're into even though they make me feel sick.

AMIRA: If you don't like'um why d'you watch them?

BROOKE: Because sometimes you do things for the people you love to make them happy!

(Beat.)

I've somehow ended up opening her Instagram page.

She's posted a story.

I shouldn't click on it, should I?

No. I really shouldn't...

She'll see I've watched it and then she'll have the upper hand.

(Beat.)

But I don't want to be left in the purgatory of wondering what she's up to—where she is—who she's with—what she's doing—if she's as devastatingly heartbroken as I am—if she's regretting it. I can't resist. I tap, and her story pops up.

(Beat.)

It's a picture of her and Lola.

They're kissing.

(A beat as it hits her.)

I'm scrolling through pictures of them together in the past trying to work out exactly when it started and I feel something, like bile, rising. This isn't how it was supposed to go. I search the cupboards for chocolate. Biscuits. I eat twelve Viennese Whirls in one sitting.

Google: 'How much sugar gives you diabetes?'

'Nose Jobs, Turkey'

'Does Face Yoga Work?'

'Is there a way to lose weight without your boobs getting smaller?'

'How to look more gay'

Message every Queer I know: 'anyone going out tonight?'

•

I'm in VFD. It's a sea of warm bodies. Sweat condensing on the ceiling above us.

Josie's already pulled and April ran into her ex so they've been having a major DMC for the last forty five minutes.

I scan the club. Again. It's reached that point in the night where anyone who wanted to pull has found someone already. Except me. I'm desperately trying to make eye contact with someone—literally anyone. And then I see them. Amira and Lola, grinding on the dance floor. The room spins. My vision blurs as I crash out of the club and on to the street. I know I mustn't cry in public, but all the fucking Ubers keep cancelling on me so I'm on the bus. Trying to hold it all in. Open Instagram. Scroll. Open WhatsApp. Scroll. Open... I need something. Anything. Anything to stop this–this feeling that I'm...

(Beat.)

I open SlideHustle. Stare at it. Then hit 'sign up'.

Maybe it's time to see if the mathematics of love can yield better results than a romcom dream

6. A NUMBER OF DATES

BROOKE: I know I'm going to rank pretty highly on the app's algorithm (thanks to white supremacy and unicorn hunters). But our consumer research showed women get fifty per cent more matches if they use a high angle selfie, flirting to the camera with a bit of cleavage on show.

So that's what I spend the next twenty minutes attempting to take in the office toilets.

If I'm going to do this, I'm going to get it right.

.

Once my profile is up, I get eleven likes within five minutes. Each one feels like a little boost.

I start getting messages: Sarah, Annais, Ben.

SARAH: Hey, nice profile.

ANNAIS: Hi! Smiley face! How are you?

BEN: You into CBT?

BROOKE: As in, the therapy?

BEN: No, Cock and Ball Torture.

BROOKE: Oh.

That's a bit forward.

.

More matches with Luke, Charlie, Suki, Roisin, Ella, Pip-

I create a spreadsheet ranking them on a number of desirables: height, politics, whether they like cheese... Anyone who scores less than ninety per cent overall I discount immediately.

Soon the spreadsheet starts to include dates and times that people are free to meet up.

.

I go on my first date later that week. I meet Sarah in a bar near her work.

She's not what I expected.

It's like the three-dimensional person I imagined from her pictures isn't the three-dimensional person stood in front of me.

I know I don't fancy her.

I'm sure I know it within the first thirty seconds.

I drink my glass of wine really quickly and wait for her to finish so I can go but...

SARAH: Shall we get another?

BROOKE: And I don't know how to say no.

SARAH: I had a great time. Let's do this again?

BROOKE: Yeah sure, I'll text you.

I never do.

•

On Thursday I meet Joel. He's attractive but honest to God the DULLEST man I've ever met, and I don't understand it because he scored 96.4% on my spreadsheet!?

•

Friday night it's Rami. 97.2% but the guy does not stop talking. Doesn't ask me a single question about myself.

•

Saturday it's MJ, 93.4%. They're nice but there's nothing there (*she points to her vagina*).

•

Sunday Evita, 95.6. Not interested.

•

Monday: Anna, Tuesday: Reuben, Wednesday: Kate, Thursday: Shaun. All of them scored over 90% but they all play out the same way. I arrive, know almost instantly I don't fancy them and sit through the rest of the date thinking 'why am I here?' but find myself incapable of leaving because I don't want to seem rude?!

•

Finally, I meet Lauren. She only scored 90.2 but she's the first person where I get that flutter in my stomach when I see her in real life.

We get really drunk on cocktails (which I post a picture of to Instagram to show I'm coping, moving on, having fun you know) and end up going dancing in Ronnie Scott's.

(Music plays. She dances. It's goofy.)

It must be two AM before we finally kiss, wet with sweat from all the dancing.

Almost immediately we're surrounded by men.

MAN 1: Damn, that's hot.

MAN 2: Kiss each other again.

MAN 1: He said, KISS EACH OTHER AGAIN.

BROOKE: I suddenly remember what it's like. Kissing another femme in public.

I think it scares Lauren off. She makes some excuse about having to get up early and leaves.

I leave her a review: 'I had a great time. Let me know if you'd like to go for another drink?'. She replies:

LAUREN: It was lovely to meet you but things are really busy right now so I'm probably not going to have time to meet up again.

BROOKE: My thirtieth is in three weeks. I'm running out of time.

I meet Raj on Monday, Cassie on Tuesday and Jay on Wednesday.

It's starting to feel like a really shit unpaid side job.

Oh God.

That's why it's called SlideHustle.

•

On Thursday I meet this guy Dave, at a comedy club in Piccadilly Circus.

I think it's a date, but I'm not sure because I'm watching him do stand up. It's one of those 'bring a friend' nights where you can only perform if you've brought someone along.

We drink too much whiskey in the bar afterwards and chat shit. Suddenly it's two AM and I'm stumbling home from the night bus, polystyrene box of cheesy chips dripping in ketchup clutched in my hand wondering what the fuck I'm doing?

I didn't even like him. His set was awful and he had this terrible habit of interrupting all my stories just before the punch line to tell his own, 'funnier' story but all he had to say was—

DAVE: Another drink? Go on... one more.

BROOKE: And I stayed. Because by this point anyone is better than nothing, right?

•

I start to wonder if it's me. The common denominator in all these shitty dates.

If each of them was an equation *I'm* the only constant factor.

•

I wake up to a missed call and a voicemail from Mum.

LUCINDA: Whatsapp says you were last online at 3:06 AM, Brooke. What were you doing? It was a Thursday night. Have you done something about that damp patch on your ceiling? And have you sorted a dress for the party yet? It's getting very close.

.

BROOKE: I'm so hungover I can barely function at work. I spend most of the morning on Instagram.

(She scrolls...)

SMUG ENGAGED WOMAN: I said YESSSSS!

SMUG NEW HOMEOWNER: Just picked up the keys to our new house. Follow @FarnhamFixerUpper to watch its transformation.

SMUG PARENT: So excited to say that today two became three as we welcome little Milo into the world. Mum and baby are doing well.

BROOKE: Make myself an espresso and text Dave because maybe we did actually have quite a nice time?

DAVE: Sorry, but I just couldn't imagine you as the mother of my child.

BROOKE: What!?

Change his rating to one star.

KATYA: Brooke?

BROOKE: Oh God.

Yes Katya?

KATYA: Have you finished the presentation deck for our pitch?

BROOKE: Not yet...

I drag myself through the rest of the afternoon, trying to finish the pitch for this God-damn app, then take myself home to get ready to meet my next date, Charlie, at a warehouse party in Hackney Wick.   24

(House music plays underneath. BROOKE tries to look like she belongs.)

The place is heaving by the time I arrive.

I've already had four G&Ts at home to take the edge off.

(shouting over the music) I'm looking for Charlie?

I say to a girl standing near the doorway. He's not answering his phone.

She points to a guy in the corner with a mullet.

HACKNEY GIRL: Try him.

BROOKE: He doesn't really look like the Charlie I've seen in his pictures, but I'm used to that by now and he's not unattractive so I approach him anyway.

(shouting) 'I'm looking for Charlie?'

COKE DEALER: *(holding out a plastic baggie)* Sure. How much do you want?

(BROOKE holds the role of the dealer for a beat before snapping out to say…)

BROOKE: Now one thing you should know about me is the closest I've ever got to taking drugs was when I used to sneak into the medicine cupboard as a child and drink the strawberry flavoured Calpol.

But standing here, on a Friday night, at a warehouse party in Hackney Wick, feeling like my life is a crock of shit, *(she shrugs)* it suddenly seems like a great idea…

(She leans over. Snorts a line of coke. Lifts her head. Nothing, and then BAM. Eyes wide. She's totally fucked.)

When it hits, I feel IN-FUCKING-CREDIBLE. Like, I am AMAZING. I am SO SEXY.

I finally find Charlie, the flesh and blood one. We take more coke and make out until we end up back at his.

•

Sat on his bed, I start to feel a bit awkward. The drugs are wearing off, and I'm not sure if I fancy him. He's actually a bit of a shit kisser.

He starts trying to pull my clothes off, but he doesn't realise I'm wearing a secret jumpsuit.

It's got this far though, so I kind of feel like I have to go through with it...

I take the jumpsuit off myself.

•

Turns out Charlie is one of those men who doesn't know what the clitoris is...

He's been thrusting for so long that I've kind of dried up. But Charlie doesn't seem to have noticed the distinct lack of lubrication and I don't really feel like I can say anything. I'm thinking it will be over soon, so the easier option is probably just to grin and bear it.

I don't know why I feel like I can't ask him to stop.

I think it's like... oh, it's like, you know when you go to the hairdressers, and you've told them what you want but they sort of ignore you and do their own thing and you start to feel a bit uncomfortable. You feel like you want to shout out 'Stop! This is shit. This is not what I asked for' but you don't wanna make a scene and it's too late now anyway. It will be over soon. They'll finish, and then you can go home and sort it out yourself.

Yeah.

That's what bad sex is like.

7. A VERY BAD COMEDOWN

(BROOKE collapses onto the floor.)

BROOKE: I spend Saturday in my pyjamas crying on the floor wondering if this is what a coke comedown feels like or if I just miss Amira.

My face is inches from the turmeric-coloured stain where the spoon of chickpea stew dropped on the floor when she kissed me.

I had a total meltdown when I realised it wouldn't wash off.

AMIRA: God Brooke, you're always such a Drama Queen.

(Beat.)

BROOKE: I get up and try to scrub it away again. I scrub and scrub until my arm aches.

Mum calls. I don't answer.

(The sound of message alert.)

LUCINDA: I've invited Harry, Julia's son, to our Ruby Wedding Anniversary-Cum-Birthday Party!

BROOKE: I wish she wouldn't call it that.

LUCINDA: He's single! He's also a property developer. Damp patch. Question mark. Dress. Question mark question mark question mark.

BROOKE: There's a picture of two origami swans attached.

What the fuck?

(texting) Please don't try to set me up with Harry.

He wears chinos. Red ones.

Maybe I could see if Amira knows a good plumber.

I search her name on WhatsApp.

She's changed her profile picture.

It's *not* the one of her and Lola anymore.

Promising.

(*texting*) Hey, how are you doing? I was just wondering if you have the number for a good plumber? Also, I really fucking miss you.

(*Beat.*)

Think I'll just delete that last bit actually...

(*She deletes 'Also, I really fucking miss you.' Then hits send.*)

Send.

Feel this thrill, followed by a pang of regret.

But she replies almost instantly!

AMIRA: I'm good thanks. Don't know any plumbers. Hope you're well. Full stop.

BROOKE: Full stop...

So, it's not a question...

But...

(*texting*) Yeah, I'm good. Do you fancy grabbing a drink one night next week. Question mark. Kiss.

She comes online. Reads the message and...

Nothing.

I wait and wait. Re-reading and obsessing.

I tried so hard. But I never really knew if I was getting it right with her.

•

Sometimes I wish I was still at school. Handing in homework and getting it back, covered in red ticks and a grade, large and circled at the top of the page, telling me how well I've done. A solid answer on my worth. Proof. Because, if you can prove yourself, if you can succeed, then everything will be alright, right?

·

Amira still hasn't responded by the time I go to bed.

I lie awake for hours thinking about her and Lola. Wondering what they're doing.

She's blocked me on Instagram which is kind of annoying cos it means I can't spy on her anymore.

8. A THIRTY-FOUR YEAR OLD VEGAN

BROOKE: When I get to the office on Monday there's a Google Calendar reminder from Katya.

KATYA: Pitch prep, 10AM, The Albatross Meeting Room.

BROOKE: All our meeting rooms are named after animals that mate for life.

That was my idea.

.

KATYA: Right team, the pitch is next week. Remember, it's all about selling the problem: the inefficient apps currently on the market. And then selling the solution: SlideHustle.

BROOKE: Right but it's not really a solution is it. I mean, the app doesn't work.

KATYA: Excuse me?

GARETH: What!?

LISA: Are you joking?

BROOKE: They all look at me. Gobsacked.

Sorry it's just. I mean, I've been using it for the last two weeks and it's just... not... working.

GARETH: Let's see.

BROOKE: Gareth grabs my phone.

GARETH: You've got loads of matches!

BROOKE: I snatch it back.

Yes, but I've been screening them all with a partner application and then ranking them on a range of variables and only 2% of them have scored over 90, and I've been on dates with all of them, and it hasn't worked out.

LISA: Yeah, but you can't rely on *just* the maths. Chemistry and physical attraction IRL isn't a quantifiable, is it? Like, what about them.

BROOKE: She points to an old match—Frankie.

They're a thirty-four year old vegan!?

LISA: What's wrong with that?

BROOKE: I just don't think I could date someone who doesn't eat cheese.

•

On the tube I open Frankie's profile again.

They're actually really fit. And they've sent me a really funny opening message

On my profile I said that I always find myself singing in the supermarket and they've said—

FRANKIE: Singing what? Clash—Lost in the supermarket?

(BROOKE snorts to herself. Then starts composing a message back.)

BROOKE: It's usually 'Pulp, Common People' which always feels a little bit ironic when I'm fondling a Butternut Squash in Waitrose.

Oh God. That was *so* middle class.

•

We arrange to meet in this new Lesbian bar on Broadway Market. It's underground. Really romantic.

My stomach clenches when I see them, and I get this wave of relief that I find them attractive in real life and not just on screen.

I mean, they are really fit, and when they look up from their phone at me, I swear all the blood rushes straight to my clit.

•

We talk about *everything*, and I feel like they're actually listening, actually interested in what *I've* got to say. And it doesn't feel like I'm on the outside it feels like I'm... IN. And when I finally look at my phone it's—

Fuck! I've gotta get the last tube.

•

And we're running through Shoreditch, laughing as we pass a pub where a load of office workers are doing karaoke and suddenly Frankie's joining in at full volume and then I'm singing too...

'Feel the rain on your skin, No one else can feel it for you!'

And I remember last year. On our way back from Mighty Hoopla, I was singing it on the tube, because Amira and me had just seen her performing it live, and she told me I was being 'too loud'. That I was embarrassing myself. And it suddenly dawns on me that maybe Amira *wasn't* my person. Maybe *this* is my person...

FRANKIE: I've had a great time. I'd like to see you again.

BROOKE: I'd like to see you again too.

And they lean in and kiss me and ugh it's magic.

•

I'm buzzing when I get home. Dancing round my flat, looking at myself in the mirror thinking 'I look alright actually'. Maybe even kind of attractive?

9. A BLOSSOMING ROMANCE

BROOKE: I wake up to a Facebook friend request from Frankie—alright Boomer—and spend the journey into work scrolling through my old photos, deleting any where I look gross before I accept it.

•

I spend the day massively resisting the urge to message them. I'm trying to concentrate at work, but my fingers keep itching towards my phone.

I keep thinking about how good they smelt last night, and how much I want to have sex with them.

•

By the time I get home I've pep talked myself into just messaging them. I'm an independent woman.

•

Friday night and we're in a pub where the bell's just rung for last orders.

FRANKIE: So... what shall we do now?

BROOKE: I don't know what comes over me, it's probably the red wine, but I decide to be very direct.

We could go back to mine and fuck?

FRANKIE: Okay. Have you got a strap? Are you into that sort of thing?

BROOKE: Yeah, but my ex took it.

FRANKIE: Wanna come back to mine then? I've got a silicone dildo, so it won't give you bacterial vaginosis.

BROOKE: I think that is the sexiest thing anyone's ever said to me...

(Something like Marvin Gaye's Let's Get It On plays. BROOKE attempts a sexy dance.)

BROOKE: They lead me into their bedroom and I'm ready to start ripping their clothes off but they say—

FRANKIE: Before we do this, is there anywhere you don't like being touched?

BROOKE: And I... I've never been asked that before.

(Beat.)

(smiling) No. You can touch me anywhere... Is there... anywhere... you don't want to be touched?

FRANKIE: Yeah. My chest. I'm gonna leave my binder on, okay?

(BROOKE nods.)

BROOKE: And I've never had sex like this before. It's fun and easy and silly and somehow, even though it's new, I'm not afraid of getting it wrong because I trust them to tell me what they want, and for the first time in my life I trust myself to say what I want too and I think, God, is this what it feels like? When you're not just... letting them do what they want to you?

10. AN INVITATION

BROOKE: In the morning they make me toast. And a cup of tea. And I look at them and think, God, I wanna have their babies.

(*to FRANKIE*) That was the best sex I've ever had.

FRANKIE: (*like there was no doubt it would be*) Yeah.

BROOKE: (*dreamy*) I start picturing all the things we might do together now... Brunch. Sunday afternoons doing a food shop for the week. Kissing on an escalator.

The kind of life we're going to build together... maybe we'll move to Margate?

I wait a whole forty-seven hours before I message them.
(*texting*) Hey, how are you? Fancy doing something again soon? Kiss kiss kiss.

Frankie comes online. Frankie's typing...

Quickly close WhatsApp so it doesn't seem like I'm waiting for their reply. And then I wait for their reply. And I wait...

Open WhatsApp again. They've gone offline. That's fine. Maybe they don't want to seem eager, replying straight away.

Put my phone away for a bit, on silent. Tell myself I won't check it until the end of Love Island: All Stars.

(*The sound of a text message alert. BROOKE leaps to check her phone.*)

Oh. It's Mum–

LUCINDA: Plumber. Question mark, question mark. Harry. Question mark, aubergine emoji, thumbs ups.

BROOKE: I think the aubergine was an accident.

·

Getting ready for bed and Frankie still hasn't replied.
I shouldn't have been so full on. Why did I put *three* kisses?

•

It's been a day now.

I can't concentrate at work. I keep checking my phone.

We were perfect together. I don't get it.

(Beat. Then it dawns on her...)

What if they got hit by a bus?

What if they were mid-responding to me as they were crossing the road, so they didn't look where they were going and just stepped out into oncoming traffic, and now they're in a coma, and none of their family know about me because we've literally been on TWO dates so I'LL NEVER KNOW, I'll just always wonder what happened?

(Beat.)

Wait a minute... I've got them on Facebook haven't I?

OK... OK. They posted yesterday afternoon. A selfie of them in some botanical garden.

Kari Manning has commented: 'Wish the afternoon had been as peaceful as it looks'.

What does *that* mean?

Click on her profile.

Oh God. She's gorgeous.

Frankie's replied to her comment, 'You loved it really. Winky face'.

WHAT. THE. FUCK?

(BROOKE puts on headphones. 'Out of Reach' plays and she mouths along to the words. It's tragi-comic, not totally tragic. She's interrupted mid song by the sound of a Google notification.)

KATYA: REMINDER, Investment pitch, 3PM in the Beaver room.

11. A DISMISSAL

BROOKE: The atmosphere in the pitch is weird. And it's not even cos of me trying not to cry. Katya keeps stumbling and stuttering over her words. I've never seen her this nervous before.

When it's my turn to speak I try to get things back on track, but I've been so busy thinking about Frankie that I haven't even planned what I'm going to say so I just waffle some nonsense about collaborative filtering and behavioural data-based algorithm learning until one of the investors interrupts me—

INVESTOR: But have you actually used the app?

BROOKE: Yeah.

INVESTOR: So, tell us about that?

BROOKE: Oh God, it's been awful! You never fancy the people that fancy you and the ones you do like end up ghosting you after you've slept together and that's just bleak and depressing and soul-destroying—*(to the audience)* It's like my brain and my tongue aren't connected.

KATYA: Gareth, run the numbers will you.

BROOKE: Katya pulls me outside.

KATYA: What the hell are you doing?

BROOKE: Sorry. It just came out.

KATYA: I want you to pack up your things and leave. Now.

12. A FLOOD

BROOKE: I spend the next three days in bed, eating Crunchy Nut Cornflakes and binge-watching F.R.I.E.N.D.S on Netflix. I know it's really homophobic, transphobic, racist, casually sexist and full of toxic masculinity, but it's still weirdly comforting.

(The sound of a text message alert.)

LUCINDA: DRESS FOR TOMORROW QUESTION MARK QUESTION MARK FIST BUMP EMOJI.

BROOKE: I thought it might have been Frankie texting.

I open our messages again. Scroll back to the top so I can analyse them all from the very beginning.

Why haven't they replied? Maybe my face looks weird when I cum.

I feel...

(She can't articulate it, so she shows us. A squeezing, pressing, fists clenched, everything crushing down.)

Didn't I do everything right?

I went to school. Worked hard. I got eleven A stars and two As in my GCSEs, and I know it makes me sound like a complete cunt but I was genuinely upset they weren't all A stars. I took my A-Levels in—

LUCINDA: Sensible subjects.

BROOKE: Went to University. I did Maths. Another sensible choice so that I could get a sensible job and buy my own flat, with my parents help, obviously.

I spent ages trying to find someone to share it all with because that's what you do.

You meet someone and you settle down and you get promoted and you upgrade your flat for a house and you have kids and you– you teach them the same. You teach them the same algorithm you followed so that they can get it right too...

So where did I go wrong?

•

I feel like I need to talk to someone, but I don't know how to admit that I need help.

I've got hundreds of friends who I never see because I always forget to reply to their texts, or they forget to reply to mine, or we can't find a time that works for both of us to meet cos I'm so busy with work and they're so busy seeing all the other people I think they secretly like more than me so I just keeping liking their posts on Instagram and watching their stories wondering why didn't I get invited to that thing and wishing I had someone, anyone who I could say: God I'm so lonely I feel like I'm marooned like there's an expanse of sea stretching for miles and miles in all directions and I just want someone to fold me in their arms and tell me it's OK but there's no-one so instead I think about how I could make myself disappear I think about chewing off my arms and legs and ripping off chunks of my stomach until the only thing left is to chew my own face off until there's no more me no more Brooke.

But there's no one I could say that to.

Everyone else is getting on with things: promotions, book publishings, doctorates, new houses, babies, engagements.

And I'm lying on my bed scrolling, as if that's going to fill this gaping hole inside of me scrolling down and down and down like I'm possessed I can't stop. My thumb keeps going flick flick flick, seeing more and more things that only make me feel more terrible about myself and the world and everything I haven't achieved and everything I should be doing better and all of the things I should be outraged about but I somehow can't find the time and I feel like the weight of it all is crushing me, like I can't breathe, like there's water rising up, like I'm drowning—wait a minute, I am drowning.

I grab my keys and I get out.

13. A DOORSTEP

BROOKE: I turn up on my parent's doorstep an hour and forty minutes later looking like a dishevelled rat.

DAD: Oh er—Brooke. Right. Just a minute, I'll get your mother.

BROOKE: He's one of those Dads who finds daughters a bit tricky.

LUCINDA: Brooke! What on earth?

BROOKE: I burst into tears.

I—I lost my job and Amira's dating someone new and they look so happy and I don't even know why I care because I met this person Frankie and it was so good—they were perfect but now they haven't replied to my text and I don't know why and I was just on Instagram and everyone else is doing so much better than I am they all look so happy and I feel so behind, and lonely, and I don't know where I went wrong and it feels mad to be even worrying about that when I look at everything else going on in the world like what is wrong with me—and then all this water started pouring in because I—I couldn't even manage to call a fucking plumber...

(BROOKE takes a ragged breath, then calms.)

She holds me, there on the doorstep. Envelops me in her arms. She smells how she always smells. Of rose geranium soap, and a hint of craft glue.

LUCINDA: Oh Brooke. You've always been very sensitive about things, haven't you?

(BROOKE recoils. Ouch. That Stung.)

14. A BIRTHDAY PARTY

BROOKE: When I wake up the next day, there's a moment before I remember... I'm thirty. Today. I don't feel any different though...

(BROOKE begins to change out of her current clothes.)...

I'm getting ready for tonight's party when Mum comes in—

LUCINDA: You're not wearing that are you?

BROOKE: Yeah? Why?

LUCINDA: It's far too short. Look I bought this—

BROOKE: She holds out the slightly too tight dress from the designer shop. The one they didn't have in a size sixteen.

LUCINDA: I let it out a bit. It should fit you now.

(Beat.)

(BROOKE looks uncertain. Then, reluctantly puts the dress on.)

BROOKE: It does. I still look like an oversized Disney Princess though.

•

At the party everyone keeps coming up to tell me how well I look. How am I? They haven't seen me in ages.

Mum has gone all out. There's a marquee and a dancefloor with a disco ball above it and the band's arrived and everyone's smiling and dancing and they all look so happy.

I drink glass after glass of Prosecco. Eventually I get a whole bottle of wine, which I take onto the dance floor with me, and soon I start to feel a little bit...fabulous.

It's my BIRTHDAY PARTY MOTHERLOVERRRSSS!

(BROOKE starts to dance unembarrassed, to something like 'I Don't Need A Man' by the Pussycat Dolls, or 'Coconuts' by Kim Petras if you want something more current.)

Clock Harry, Julia's son. He's wearing his red chinos, standing alone, pint in hand, looking a little lost. Shimmy my way over to him, grab him by the tie and drag him onto the dance floor.

(She dances enthusiastically with him, uninhibited.)

I'm really getting into it, trying to tug Harry's tie off when I feel a hand on my arm, and a whisper, sharp in my ear—

LUCINDA: Brooke. I think that's probably a bit much, for tonight.

(Everything stops. Expands out, crashes back in.)

BROOKE: I stop. De ja vu. There's this familiar tightening in my chest. I can't breathe.

I burst out of the marquee and onto the lawn outside.

I'm running now. Down to the bottom of the garden where it backs on to the woods. There's this tree I used to climb as a kid. If you shuffle along one of the middle branches you can drop down into the woods. I land arse first in the mud.

This can't be it, can it? Everything I thought I'd be by now, everything I thought I'd have. Gone.

I go to check my phone for the millionth time today, to see if Frankie's replied to my text, forgetting that I don't have it on me. Women's clothes don't have pockets so it's lying in a stupid clutch bag somewhere on a table in the marquee.

I haven't been able to get Frankie out of my head. How could something so perfect just dissolve into nothing? I don't understand *why*. If they could just explain it. If they could just tell me why then maybe I could move on.

I'm stomping through the woods now.

It doesn't make sense.

Off the path. Stumbling on tree roots in the dark.

Why didn't they text me back?

Pushing past branches.

We were literally perfect together. You don't have sex like that and then *never* speak to the person again, do you? And it wasn't just the sex it was everything. It was how easy it was to talk to them and how much they made me laugh and that butterfly feeling in my stomach when I looked at them and the way I could have melted into their chocolate brown eyes when they were lying above me. It was everything that relationship could have been if they'd just given me a chance!? I just need them to give me a chance because I really feel like I could be exactly what they want if they just told me how to be exactly what they want.

(Beat.)

(BROOKE hears it. She hears the madness of what she's just said...)

Oh my God.

That's me isn't it.

I've spent my whole life trying to be what I think other people want me to be. Trying to get it right. Trying to be the perfect student, the perfect daughter, the perfect girlfriend, the perfect bisexual and I'm actually just lost.

(BROOKE looks around her.)

I'm lost. In the fucking woods. Alone. On my thirtieth birthday.

(Beat.)

It's almost dark now.

I walk back the way I think I came. I can't see anything familiar. Every tree looks the same. And I'm sure I can feel someone watching me. In the trees. But every time I whip around to look behind me, no one's there. I speed up. Running now. Barefoot, landing on branches that scatter the floor. Trying to find the path. The sound of an owl behind and I speed up to a sprint because what if it's a man pretending to be an owl and he's telling his accomplice in some sort of owly morse code which direction I'm running in and it would be just my fucking luck to get murdered tonight so I run and run and run, legs burning and my lungs screaming at me to stop until there it is: the path.

Still running until I hit the road at the end, where I can circle back along it to my house.

Sweaty. Red faced. Out of breath. Mud on my dress. Twigs in my hair. Bare feet sore. But I'm fine. Back at my house. And I'm totally fine.

15. ANOTHER ENDING

LUCINDA: Where have you been!? You missed the cake! Look at the state of you—you're covered in mud—

BROOKE: Mum, stop. Stop.

(Beat.)

I need you to just let me be me. Okay?

LUCINDA: What are you talking about? Of course you can be you!

BROOKE: No. No. You're always telling me what to do. What to wear, how to act. Telling me to lose weight—and I'm not even fat, but even if I was my body and what I do with it isn't any of your business—

LUCINDA: I don't think you're fat—

BROOKE: You judge me all the time and I don't need it because I'm already judging myself constantly. And it's exhausting.

LUCINDA: I'm not judging you.

BROOKE: Well, that's what it feels like. When you say those things to me.

(Beat.)

LUCINDA: I never meant—I just want the best for you.

BROOKE: But it's your version of the best for me. And I don't want to keep chasing something that isn't mine. Chasing some mad promise of what I could be if I just tried harder or what I could have if I just wasn't me. What a waste of energy. Constantly trying to fix something that isn't even broken. Think of all the things that are *actually* broken that we could fix if we weren't constantly worrying about being perfect.

(Beat.)

I look up at her and she's staring at me like... Like this is me *and* this is her, and we've both spent our entire lives reaching for a level of perfection that doesn't even exist.

(They see each other. For the first time.)

LUCINDA: I love you so much Brooke, and I'm sorry that I've made you feel like you aren't good enough.

(Beat.)

(BROOKE nods. She gets it.)

BROOKE: I love you too. Probably more than anyone else in the world.

(Beat.)

(They look at each other.)

LUCINDA: Oh, I er—I got you something actually. I forgot to give it to you earlier.

BROOKE: I pull off the wrapping and open the box. It's a mug which says, 'You Do You'.

LUCINDA: Seems a bit silly now.

(BROOKE looks at the mug. Laughs.)

BROOKE: It is very silly. But I love it. Thanks.

(Beat.)

I think about it as we go back inside.
'You Do You'...
I'm not sure I know exactly what 'me doing me' is yet. But whatever it is, it isn't this hideous dress.

(BROOKE takes the dress off and pulls on a baggy T-Shirt instead.)

(She gets out a karaoke mic.)

(She presses play on the machine.)

(The Karaoke backing track to 'Unwritten' by Natasha Bedingfield plays.)

(She sings.)

(Pure Joy.)

THE END

Algorithms is available as an Audible Original Recording Audiobook starring Sadie Clark as Brooke, Alison Steadman as Lucinda, Seyan Sarvan as Amira, Len Gwyn as Frankie, Desiree Burch as Katya, Ciara Baxendale as Josie, Joe Thomas as Charlie and an ensemble cast.

Directed by Lisa Spirling with original score by Tawiah.

Length: 2 hrs and 38 mins

Algorithms is intended for an adult audience as it contains scenes of an explicit sexual nature and strong language. Listener discretion is advised.

ALSO AVAILABLE FROM SALAMANDER STREET

All Salamander Street plays can be bought in bulk at a discount for performance or study. Contact info@salamanderstreet.com to enquire about performance licenses.

COWBOYS AND LESBIANS by Billie Esplen
ISBN: 9781914228902
Charming, queer romantic comedy about British schoolfriends writing a parody American coming-of-age romance.

SHE by Anthony Clark
ISBN: 9781739103057
Seven short plays charting the experiences of different women from childhood to old age, these stories, each with an intriguing twist, are visceral, poignant and laced with humour.

FATTY FAT FAT by Katie Greenall
ISBN: 9781913630744
A funny, frank and provocative show about living in a body the world tells you to hate.

these words that'll linger like ghosts till the day i drop down dead by Georgie Bailey
ISBN: 9781914228896
An experimental play for two actors that explores the things we wish we'd said to those who have left.

AD LIBIDO by Fran Bushe
ISBN: 9781914228476
Fran Bushe's hilarious' quest (with songs) for a satisfying sex life.

FUNNY PECULIAR and SIEGE by Vici Wreford-Sinnott
ISBN: 9781914228063
Powerful monologues with exciting new disabled women protagonists.

www.salamanderstreet.com